Sweet Like CINNAMON

A Compilation of 50 Poems

KASHVIE SAXENA

INDIA • SINGAPORE • MALAYSIA

ISBN
Paperback 979-8-89673-474-1
Hardcase 979-8-89744-292-8

For my parents, saambu & rehaan

Prologue

I once read that each poet has an emotion that all their writing revolves around. Richard Siken's is thought to be panic, Sylvia Plath's to be around despair about self acceptance, Emily Dickinson's was mainly introspective works contemplating existence and Franz Kafka wrote around anxiety and self loathing.

Dear reader, I wouldn't dream of claiming to be equivalent to them, but I am, to my very core, a poet. Poetry is my emotional support system that I turn to when the toll of life becomes rather unbearable for me. Don't get me wrong, I'm a happy healthy child. My family makes me happier than I can express, my friends goof around the way any teenagers would, and I have everything I could possibly need. I just write in an exaggerated manner; to express, to tell, to create. I write to be okay.

Do be humble when you begin reading, take it in like a journey. You'll see the world through the eyes of my 9-year-old self in the first few poems slowly mature into my current views. It grows, it changes, it is almost alive.

The book you are holding is a compilation of my less than flattering moments, my verses of dramatised sorrow and a whole lot of hope with which i have sent these out into the world. The poetry you are about to read has a central emotion too and I would want you to decide what it is for yourself.

Dearest gentle reader,

Do not delve too deep into my miseries, just enough to know that you are not alone.

With all my love,
Hope, trust & pixie dust,
Kashvie Saxena

"And so, being young
And dipped in folly
I fell in love with melancholy"

Edgar Allen Poe

(I suggest you start at the end)

Contents

The Earlier Early Years

#1

An Ode to The After

The first month spent in disbelief
Of realisation of change
All refusals to accept
This life rearranged

Second month is sorrow
Over the final decision to leave
The truth has been accepted
There are no more tricks up the sleeve

Third month is living, truly living
With no regrets and just enjoying
Make the best of the time left
This slow sort of dying

Fourth month is love
To be grateful beyond perception
To spend all that is left with the ones who matter
A month of exceptions

Fifth is happy
To start an adventure
Meet new and cherish old
To fate we surrender

Sixth is nostalgic
For times gone and memories lost
To remember and weep
And learn of time the true cost

Seventh is goodbye
Goodbye to the memories and moments of laughter
To the friends and enemies
Goodbye I'll say and find an new happily ever after

#2

The beach

I stood staring at the sea
shells on the shore
I see millions of fish and I'm
sure there are plenty more

Whilst living in a world
with sorrows and tears
There's still flowers around
Despite the cities that have drowned

The sand, salty sea and sun
surely lift my spirits
The night is silent
Besides the sad quiet whispers of lyrics

#3

Dried or died

Mid creation, the ink ran out
No more love or loss, just a drought
I wonder why
Why why why, did my creativity die

Yes, it was just the ink that dried
Oh yes, just the tears that I've cried
Just the days and hours I spent
And with this ink, they all went

My eyes have lost their glow
Dreams gone through a light blow
The magic is all gone
The glaze of joy now torn

Mid creation, the ink ran out
Gone gone gone, the genius withdrawn
With this ink, dies that dream
Gone, unheard & unseen

#4

A dream long gone
but not forgotten
A friend long lost
like a cotton field with no cotton

Yes, loss brings pain
but loss of something you never had
Is perhaps a gain

Gain to the list
of people who left
Gain to the little
pain I've kept

A loss is gained
to the heart that pained

Today I've lost a friend
Deep down though I knew
All things must end.

#5

The Countdown

The seconds count down
It's time to study in a couple of them
The minutes go by
& To class youre condemned

The hours count down
It's time for school in some
The days go by
And emotions go numb

The months count down
It's time for exams in a bit
The years go by
And to some job you commit

What you didn't see
While all this time went, working, studying, worrying
Your childhood is now gone
And those empty days, minutes and months of study
are the only thing you've won

#6

"Once upon a time"
I read about a story that's now mine
I see the wolf of greed and the queen of vain
These characters bringing about happiness and pain

I see the happy beginning, the sorrowful middle and
the unfinished end
I think of how I made and lost each friend
So many people affected
Yet not the ones I expected

The story seems like a fairy tale
Fantastical, all the things accomplished and failed
I can relate indeed
Although I'm not in this tale, I live what I read

I watch betrayals take place
And witness loyalty's grace
People come and go in every chapter
All leading towards their happily ever after

#7

Time is of essence
dear time, I miss it's presence
Time I've lost
I look back at streets I crossed

my watch lays broken in shatters
it's needles long, still ignorant of all matters
I see my life as it's been
I think of how I lost and how to win

Time, time it is the answer
this clever, skilled dancer
time it is what I need
To win at last, finish my task, to succeed

the glass seems to float through the air
each piece fitting fair and square
the needles resume their ticking
It seems I have got my time, I start living

#8

All these lyrics I recite
Every key term I highlight
Everything I wear
Or do with my hair
Every person I meet
A new identity I seek
Any way to change who I am

So I change
I put the real me back in a cage
For every person, a new me I create
Secretly harbouring my hate
I cry to myself and if someone sees
I lie but never freeze
I create yet another facade
Soon whom my "friends" will discard

The sun comes up and it goes down
In more and more personalities I drown
And at the end of the day
All these nameless faces I see
And faceless names I know
They're all for nothing but show

#9

the highlighter

A textbook and it's contents i highlight
Each term, left to right
I tape classes over my memories
Forget what freedom feels like; a summer breeze

I highlight further on, soldiering on
Forgetting precious things now long gone
I am highlighting: memorising
I am replacing, erasing.

Read, re read
Plant each seed you'll need
Although my thought scatters
sanity in tatters

This highlighter
In the hands of yet another fighter.

#10

I'll save time by keeping it to myself
I'll save feelings by not asking for help
He's there but can't see
And I'm somewhere im not supposed to be

I'll save money by not going to therapy
I'll wipe my tears on my clothes to save every single tree
She's close but so far away
We exchange three words each day

Words flash through my mind
Haunting memories I'll rewind
You and me against the world
But what if you're my world, so the story turned

What once was mine
People lost in time
Lonely but never alone
Meaningless notifications on my phone

I'll save all I can for no fee
But when I'm drowning alone
Who's saving me.

The Miseries of A Dramatised Human

#11

Adding to
collections of dark circles
Adding to
reserves of wasted potential
I didn't know
But you? You didn't understand.
now look
where
we've come
(hand) in (hand)

It's all your fault. You killed it. You killed me. When
you left.

why
did you leave
me
alone
to fight demons

That weren't even mine to begin with...

#12

hidden

people, most always, do the right thing
Out of guilt not good will
I'm left on seen until I'm crying
every cell in my brain is defying
'I'm trying you know' I'll say
'So what' they'll reply, 'everyone does. make your own way'
But what if I'm not good enough for that
What if I'm just not
I'll look up words when I can't find a rhyme
How on earth do I make a path for myself that too in time
I cheat I lie I hide it and I cry
And all I ever really do is ask myself why
I'm laying on the bed of an ocean of my lies and my tears
My insecurities and fears
What if I can't seem to resurface

And I just want to stay in a case
Or maybe not stay at all
So I lay here
After the highs I've ridden
Now at my eternal low, only wanting to stay
forever hidden.

#13

It's not that I miss the place
Or the people even
In truth I miss the time
The way we'd rhyme

I miss the jokes
The bond
The sun rays
I miss those days.

I miss the looks
The way we sat
I miss who we where
What we had

I can still text them
Ask about their days
Where I have no place

They'll laugh at new jokes
And I won't understand
I'll walk through the sun now
But they won't be there to hold my hand

Maybe I miss who we were
Not who we've become
I miss those days
when I felt right, when i was someone

#14

She has a new pfp
A new hairdo
She listens to songs i never knew
Her clothes seem brighter
The bags under her eyes lighter
She tells me shes happier

She tells me about her day
But i no longer know the right thing to say
We plan days to meet
Where we can run wild, free on any street
We dream
But we know it wont happen, despite how we're so
very keen
Yeah she's happier these days

I built her the bridge over troubled waters
We hid away from the plotters
But bridges are meant to be crossed
Left behind, lost
Yeah she's happier these days

I listen to the songs she'd told me
Re watch movies she'd once showed me
I think about the jokes we had
Silly things over which we'd be sad
Yeah she's happier these days
And I think
We're just headed for different ways

#15

Anaphora

I've come to learn
I like used books
not ones with highlighted hearts in nooks
the ones with folded pages
& worn out edges
I've come to learn
They feel more like home
New books with straight covers feel to me like an
empty ice cream cone
Hollow and strong
not touched in so very long
I like used books
The ones I can hug and cry over
Not worried about colours fading from the cover
I've come to learn
I like used books

#16

The Waves Will Never Stop

you don't realise when you stop talking to your
"best friends"
Or when you start forgetting the lyrics to your
favourite song
You don't realise when the tunes start mixing
together
Leaving blanks in space of words
You don't realise when comfort food stops giving
comfort
Or when happiness becomes a luxury
You don't realise when nights become sleepless
Or when thoughts become poison
Until one day it hits you strong and sudden
Like a wave a lonely shore
You can't do anything about it, no you just have to
fight. Always be ready for more

#17

The trains cross
whoosh by, yet
Two hands joot out
One from each train
The grilled windows
They meet
Along with their eyes
And hearts skip a beat
They can feel it, if only for a moment
This is their world for all outside is false and
unknown
They are one yet so different
alas parallel lines don't bend
So they see they glance but then
The trains begin to leave
That was the only time I felt able to breathe
The trains whoosh away
And empty rail roads lay
That was how I'd felt
When I met that girl
yellow blue headphones
Ceramic sculptures and deep poems

She'd smile when her hair curled
We'd meet and to the tunes spin and whirl
That was how I'd felt when I'd met that girl
With a love for street artists and people of the world
Odd songs and books
But then she'd been whooshed away
Leaving me alone
Knowing my world is there
Living happy and all I can do
Is stare
At empty rail roads
Letters with deciphered notes
Empty rail roads

#18
*speakers - alec Benjamin

Old Papers

I am sitting among old papers
Half filled with thoughts of mine
Scattered through time
Stories and songs
Hinting at laughs and fights
Tales of fear and might
innocence and dreams
Hopes lost and imaginary scenes
Tears and hugs
Hot summers and winters with chocolate filled mugs
And then I think
What I write now
Will soon be "old papers"
Scattered through time
So I laugh as loud as I can
And have fears to face
Show my might in every race
I dream as much as I can
Hope for every little plan

I fight and leave and return
Shove and hug and learn
Because what I live now
Will soon be old papers
Scattered through time
And I'd like them to remember what once was mine

#19

Title: Resignation to jeybliuyb4TI

I write this
Regret filling me
I write this
Thoughts killing me
I write this repeating words I've used a thousand times
Because they are my escape
From my mind.
I write this to inform you,
Although i am yet to find out who i am addressing this to,
That i hereby resign.
My post, my job
As a living being
I shall continue to fulfil
My responsibilities as a child
To study, score trying to get somewhere in life
But i shall no longer be alive
Not in the sense my body lays cold

Rather in the one where my heart hides away its gold
I write this
As a treasure map
To one day find that gold
To inform you
I tried; alas this is the consequence of when i could
not anymore
I write this
To inform that i shall still
Ask when one does not smile
And hear them out for a while
However i do this as a shell
Existing in an waterless well
Asking only
For the sake of these beautiful beings
Still alive and full of dreams
So they do not end up like me
No sir, they are not worthy of that i deem
I sit here
Writing
Typing
Wasting time
For this endless rhyme
Because i know when it ends

My death will have begun
And while i would avoid it if i could
Here i am
Desperately, desolately
Writing to inform you that
Dear stranger
I thereby
Resign.

#20

My Favourite Room

I remember that room
My favourite in the world
It held the sun and the moon
All at once
All through you
I remember its door
Childish and innocent
Covered with planet stickers
I should have known even a strong flame flickers
I remember
Its warmth and love
Filled with understanding and trust
Laughter and hugs
Calls and late night talks
Holding hands and early morning walks
Jokes and teasing
Hearts ever pleasing
Minds intertwined
Wind chimes danced and chimed
I remember slowly watching dust settle

In my favourite room.
Cover all good.
Webs appeared;
Understanding disappeared
I remember when it started feeling cold,
Heavy.
I held on.
But I remember leaving that room
Seeing the door one last time
The treasures inside stuck, no longer mine
It's been a while i suppose
I can't quite figure out where the piece that is
me goes
I keep reaching for that door
Knocking hopelessly at walls, searching for more
I try but it stays out of view
And i realise
All along,
My favourite room
Was just you.

#21

Dead poets society

It breaks my heart to see doors locked
Despite that i never open mine
Breaks my heart to see you leave
Behind your potential your greatness

It breaks my heart to see pages not folded
Because now no one will remember
Breaks my heart to see what you could've been
To see broken fragments of beautiful dreams

It breaks my heart to see no spark in your eyes
To see you've stopped questioning why
Breaks my heart to see empty pages
That you'll never fill now

It breaks my heart to mark out days you've been gone
To see you become just another pawn
Breaks my heart to see you fight till you give up
And how it doesn't even affect all these corrupt

It breaks my heart not see you anymore
Yet as I watch them fight and disagree
All i can think is how
It breaks my heart
To know that you've left me.

#22

(Stay) Left

when you think they're gone
but you have no proof.
they sit with you and talk.
not knowing you knew.

they smile and laugh
but you see it in their eyes.
your heart is left in half &
they keep up the facade

and you do too
because you're scared of what would happen if they
knew you knew.

they've stopped listening as carefully
or meaning things truly
their eyes wander when they claim their love
and with every lie you think you've had enough.

but what can you do

what can you say
that they've not been acting the same way?
what if they leave
and you're all alone
and it's no one's fault but your own

so you sit in silence in the web of lies,
where nothing is true.
all because you wouldn't be able to bear
if they knew that you knew too.

#23

GENZ

we call ourselves genz
but we can't say a complete word as you can see
We call ourselves genz
But we mean nothing genuinely
We call ourselves genz
But don't let the thought of the last generation trick
you into thinking we're free
We call ourselves genz
The last, the best, the most coping with stress
We lie, cheat and constantly hate
But of course act like it's a piece of cake
What we really are is just liars
But we call ourselves genz
And once you're a part of us, you can never not be.

The Internal Cogs & Workings Of *Adolescence*

#24

Robert Frost Was Right When He Said *"Nothing gold can stay"*

Our status has been set to away
On Google chat
We've moved on to phones & Instagram traps
We used to catch each other on different days
Ones where we were sad
Ones where we had joy like we've never had
Growing up is odd
It's exciting it's upsetting
I dont want to study for boards
I want to be young and pretty
But im not ready to let go of my plastic swords
I dress myself up instead of my barbie's
But i miss seeing fairies in all the trees
I make sculptures that amaze and impress
But i liked the funny looking princess with the play
    doh dress
I've started liking the dark
But i miss my smiling kite lamp and its spark

It feels so scary getting old
I think about when my friends will all have kids of
their own to scold
They'll play with food and laugh themselves silly
Blow bubbles in their drinks and fall asleep on
the couch
They wont believe us when we say its scary to
grow old
But soon enough their energetic run will disappear
into a tired slouch
We'll look through old albums, all the memories and
emotions they hold
And now those kids will think, just like we once did
It feels so scary getting old
It feels so scary, getting old

#25

Rain Rain Rendition

Rain rain go away
When did we part ways?
Rain rain, Come again another day
Im held back with words I couldn't say
We want to play
But to mind games we fall prey
Rain rain go away

Turned into please don't leave me, please stay

Rain rain please stay
Keep my tears company, let the sky be like my room,
walls of grey
Rain rain
Inside and out
Never let me see another day of drought
Rain rain
Until the world washes away its pain
Let it rain rain.

#26

The Cheshire Cat Syndrome

All is good with my health
But within me lays a corpse
In my isolation, all of reality warps
All is well with my immunity
But my defences begin to fall
All is well with my body
But my eyes say it all.
Im sick i say
But they dont see it my way
Im sick, not in my blood
But in my mind deep within
Drip drip
Seconds fall away
Does it matter if i call ?
Sand is time
Falling away and pulling me in
It doesn't matter if i win
I feel it slip away.
The fear of what others will say
Colours and shapes lose meaning
I know i am alone when there is no difference
between reality and & dreaming

#27

The PuZZle of Yin & Yan

She liked pretty dolls and boys
I played with mud and toys
She put clips in her hair
And i scared her with my glare :)
She made a mess and talked a lot
While i kept to myself and did not
But at the end we played together
In a funny mix of her and me
It's my favourite place to be
Where she is loud and i am quiet
Late at night it's a riot
Yin and yan at its peak
Our own language we speak
We're different as can be
Yet i love her more than i could ever love me

#28

thoughts & deluded poison

At the end of the day
It's my thoughts that comfort me.
Comfort me when the witches have flown
Comfort me when the letters I wrote you have
been thrown

They will judge me
Tear apart my face, my hair
But they can't take what they can't see
The can't take my thoughts from me.

They'll laugh and mock
Or maybe they wont talk
But my thoughts will remain
To poison me and then take away the pain

Oh yes it sounds terrible!
Terrible as can be.
But what else is a girl to do
When she is as lonely as me.

It's my thoughts that comfort me so im not alone
It's my thoughts that comfort me
So im not cold to the bone
It's my thoughts that i call home

#29

NIRVANA

I know a girl
Who's smile is the most beautiful in the world
I know a girl
Who's hair flies around, and though its not Barbie
straight, it's curiously curled
I know a girl
Who's as sweet as can be
She never worries
And sees the best in me
I know a girl
Who embodies kindness
And her eyes are timeless
She doesn't let others decide her worth
Her words are like a hearth
I know a girl
Who's beautiful inside out
She's someone i couldnt to live without
I know a girl who's as happy as can be
Only thing is, i dont see her much while she's hiding
within me.

#30

Wildflower ~ beach house

I lay sunbathed
On the bed
All dressed up & ready
Ready for a day that won't ever come.

Mind filled with words
For a phone call
That'll never ring
Body ready for an embrace
That'll never walk through the front door.

It's the sad sinking truth
Of waiting for something that'll never come
Like standing at a train station
Shut years back
Just like laying on my bed
Waiting for people I never met
Waiting
For a life i never even had

#31

Woods

Let's take a walk
You & me
Come along, along with me
Lets talk about what we could've been
Come along, talk with me
Leave the chaos
The churning sea
Come along, to the woods with me
For a while, maybe an hour or two
Under the light we can be true
Come along, through the tall trees
Remember when we were last here, they were
just seeds
Come along, visit what we'd been
Come along, come walk with me
Let's walk in the footprints we left behind
Come along, away from where you are confined
Take a walk through these woods with me
Notice what all has come to be

Since you last visited these woods, since you last even
thought of me
We're taking our walk through these woods
Away from the bright buzz of the crowded city
Our journey is timeless it seems
Away from plotting of schemes
Stop your running it is not a race
Stop and look at your face
Are you who you wanted to be
Or as far from it as can be?
Stop your running and take a walk with me
A walk through the woods
The question I hope to convey
What are these woods in your life
Why do you remain with those who stray and betray
Why is it that from these woods you stay away?
Im sure you are running now, you have someplace
to be
But i do hope you'll soon return to the woods
& come take a walk with me

#32

red perfume

On my desk,
My old, empty perfume bottle lays.
It's red glass clear and hollow
Within the scent & memories linger
The mark of a ring that used to stay on my finger

Perhaps you don't remember the jokes they made
But you remember that they were the funniest to you
Perhaps you dont remember the exact shade of
their eyes
But you remember how you felt when they looked
towards you

Perhaps there is no more perfume for the bottle
to give
But perhaps just the bottle is enough to relive
Maybe you don't need a glass full
Maybe just the presence of the glass is enough
To remind you
of what all has been

#33

The Time Fate Met Coincidence

The time fate met coincidence
Some said it was fate who set it up
Others it was by mere coincidence or luck

Coincidence acted surprised
While fate flirted and acted sly
Coincidence joked and smiled
Fate burst out with laughter her eyes wide like a child

Fate knew it was meant to be
Coincidence thought it was by chance
But they danced a little dance
Then coincidence had to leave
Fate stayed knowing well how the story would weave

Coincidence returned perhaps because he couldn't
stop thinking of fate
Or maybe he wasn't thinking so late
Maybe he returned because he forgot his wallet

He met her again and they left together did you
call it?
Was the wallet fate
Or was it coincidence
Or was it something else making it all fit like a glove?
I think the mastermind, the true connection was
really just love

#34

What a funny girl i am
Searching for the pens I've stuck in my hair
Falling on the floor as if slipping on stairs
What a funny girl i am indeed
to see walls in front and walk into them still
You'd laugh if you knew, i know one day i will
To see what a funny girl i am
For turning off the WiFi and wondering why my
Pinterest wont work
For putting paper bags on my head
And having a silly little routine before bed
What a funny girl i am indeed
For hating coffee and sipping on sugar and ice
For saying i hate rats but i like mice
Only because they made Cinderella's dress
Oh! I am such a mess!
But i do suppose it is what makes me me
The falling-off glasses and the scraped up knee
I like to think
That someday someone may ask
What was she like? And then you may say
What a funny girl she was
And tell them tales of the little things i did with no
real cause

#35

63 MARKS

Shorts are something I've always hated.
Because of how they expose my carefully kept facade
I dont like to admit what i did, the monster I've created.
I can only look down and see
Some 63 marks all over me.

It does not then matter
How well i highlight my eyes
Because i can no longer disguise
And i am once again reduced to these 63 marks
Each like a hit to the heart.

I see their eyes glance down and run away
They fret and gossip and wonder
I stand there with nothing quite left to say
Because they do not hear me
Over my 63 marks.

I can never seem to escape the long road of remarks
All over my 63 marks.

#36

Rebooted Boot Theory

It's pure delusion and madness and i adore it
It is dancing alone in the kitchen
And seeing coloured lights and a roaring crowd
It's singing into the spatula and being quiet
 pretending to be loud
It's wild and bright and secret

It's shining fame and glamorous hair
When the reflection is really just a Barbie night suit
 but you dont care
It's simple and special
It's dancing alone in the kitchen
When everyone is asleep
And your heart jumping out at you
And you should probably reply to the ten emails,
 eight texts and three calls
But the crowd adores you
So you keep
Dancing alone in the kitchen

It's a real dream or a dream real
Does that make sense? It's surreal
The words mix and your vision blurs after you've
abandoned your glasses
But you sing along to ABBA and Elton John
As if they aren't whispers in your AirPods
But all your inhibitions have gone
When you are dancing alone in the kitchen
You're an octopus and a penguin
The camera makes you look deranged but the
reflection in the fan says otherwise
And you sway and throw your hands up
When you look around
You may see a single light on in
Some far away building
And a figure dancing
Alone in their kitchen
Their hair flying and just maybe if your eyes meet
And *everybody loves somebody* begins to play
There may be a time where you
Will be with someone
In the dead of night
Dancing alone in your kitchen
In secret in front of the world

The meaning here has been twisted and twirled
You may just understand if you
Wait until the sun hides away
And in your kitchen alone you sway

#37

12 PAGE ANSWER BOOKLET

Write in black or dark blue ink
HB pencil may be used for any diagram or
graph only
Write your name, centre number and candidate
number in the boxes above
Watch as they fit us into these boxes

I despise the metallic scent embedded within each
strand of my skin
My hands marred by compass scars and pencil marks
You forged me
In your burning world
Burned until my blood curled.

Your cold, shiny awards gawk and mock me
But sure, hand me
A prize
For every bit
I sacrifice.
And the day I won first

I thought it'd quench my thirst
And yet I found
Its hollow fake plastic was never worth anything
    i lost.

On the drive home
I lost myself
Between my mother tongue
And the language they taught me in school
Till all my words
Were a poor translation of incoherent thoughts.
Till my reality was shattered in shards.
On the drive home
i lost myself
Between the child I was
And the student they taught me to be
Till my face was half half
Teary eyes and a laugh.

Fit your life into
The twelve-page answer booklet.

#38

Two Ice Cubes & Soda

avoiding my eyes
she pours ice and soda over the golden liquid
claiming
'It's all better now ; there's nothing to it
There's barely any in this'
It's all ice and soda.

tell me
if I poured you half glass of poison
And then dropped in some ice
Is it not
still
the same
is it not still the thing that brings you closer to
the end..

But sure, draw the curtain over my eyes
And Cover it with your lies
Your two ice cubes and soda
You drown in the mix and climb highs

My beautiful child;
I can't quite recall when her innocence died
Perhaps somewhere
It drowned
in those two ice cubes and soda
I look around
And see my girl nowhere to be found

#39
no surprises

bells

The doorbell echos its soft tune
To which our ears have grown immune
The clock ticks away
Minutes are money, trade each day

Just sometimes, when the thunder calls
I feel silence through the crowded halls
Just sometimes, when the sky is pouring
My mind isn't roaring

When my feet feel the ground
I dont think about the horrors we've found
When my eyes notice the clouds move
I dont feel anyone disapprove

When my hands run across flowers
I dont feel the need to plan my hours
When the wind hugs my face
I dont think to maintain my grace

Please let me dissolve
Into the little moments, where i find my resolve
Where the birds chatter and the leaves swaying is all
    i can hear
And there's no prying eyes near

Let me dissolve
Into the raindrops & tree tops
Into the odd shaped clouds
Let me disappear
Into the soil from which i came
Into the ground and there let me remain
So that i can at last be here, there & somehow
    nowhere

#40
back to the old house

SMITHS

"I love the smiths"
But you only ever listen to their hits
Here comes the sun
But where were you when there was *no one*?

In a fast paced world
You try to be faster
But silly girl, you forgot
The faster you go, the lesser you know

The faster you leave,
The less you'll ever see
The faster you hear
Lesser truth will appear

A different song each day
But do you know what any of them say
Did you ever stop to listen
Or stop to watch the tree tops glisten

Did you ever watch cars pass by
Rather than race for a couple moments of a high
Did you ever feel the sunset soak into your bones
Instead of scrolling instantly on your phones

The social circles we run in
Why is it a race no one can win
Yet you keep chasing round and round
And for what to be found

Step out the circle
Stop running
Stop rushing
Stop.

"I love the smiths"

So then pave me the road they walked on

Show me where they got lost from

Instead of replying with "sorry?"

Show me the light that never goes out.

{There Will Always Be a Before, And an After}

{You've seen the before, now here is what was left}

After

#41

aBStrAcT

I reached for my toy
But that is when i realised
It's not there
And it hasn't been for quite some time

It slipped away between the to do lists and classes
Nameless amongst the masses
I sit at home
Longing for home beyond the walls surrounding me
Beyond the masks, there's nothing i can see
Empty actors they're all part of a play
I watch them day after day
The curtains never close
And the show never ends
The crowd wont applaud
They'll play on loop a show you never chose
My eyes are bloodshot
And ears are aching
My mind sick and tired of faking
Just look me in the eye

And let me see beyond
The fake lashes and question why
I want to go home
Where my toy will accompany me so im never alone
Where i dont hear lies day and night
Or at least none i can decipher
Where I didn't have to spend every second to fight
I miss when falling asleep in a strange place
Would mean waking up in bed
And not watching the consequences unravel in
your head
I want my toy

#42

I look out
To beyond the ledge
Blurry visions fill my head
Something roars into my face
I'm standing on the edge
Without the confidence to give in
Or go back as a disgrace
Paralysed by indecision I stay on the sliver of ground
Head pounding for a solutyuon that can't quite
be found
Standing on the edge
But which is it
Edge of a knife
Edge of a cliff
Or is it just the edge of my life
Or perhaps its very end,
today & maybe this very night
If I were not stuck alone with fright
What goes in
What goes out
The words that come out my mouth
I do not recognise

I'm scared, frightened beyond my wit
Getting weaker with every hit
One toward the edge
And three backward
Four in front
I'm back again isn't it absurd

#43
o superman

moderntech

Please help
Im trying to connect
But the network is glitching
I want some constant
But their sides are always switching.

I hate my device.
It connects to me in such a disconnected way
That i feel it go through me, its in the name, its a vice
Please just help me
Get through the day.

Warm loving home
Filled with
Cold, hard screens
The world right here, each alone.
So connected, so modern,
So in love with damn machines.

Please help me
Put away these barriers
Just be.
Come meet me like long forgotten couriers ?

Im consuming so much
Through my devices
And in this "immersive" experience surrounded
by (de)vices
It feels more
Like they
Are consuming me.

#44

dRoWn

I never learnt how to swim
So water was never my favourite
And drowning always scared me
But never like it did when i sat alone
And the tears filled up way beyond my bones

In
Large
Crashing
Waves

You and i were only just
Counting
Our
Days

And the day that you left

My life jacket
You kept

As the tears filled up

And my vision blurred

I saw you smile

And "i love you"

Was the last thing

I ever heard.

#45

Green, Green, Grass

And when death shall embrace me
I shall tell it of all it didn't have
When the colour leaves my face
I'll remember the colours of the sky
When my heart stops beating
I'll remember who i gave it to
When my eyes no longer blink
I'll watch my love in my mind
When my soul leaves my body
I'll remember how i used to run
Memories, like wisps of smoke
And the final time i spoke
But now i'll fly
Away with death
And just perhaps the day death shall embrace me is
    the day I'll fall in love with living

#46

2 bracelets

I've always slept on the right side of the bed
But now I'll sleep in the middle
And I guess since we were little
I always knew
You'd leave one day but it never seemed so soon

I used to have one cupboard
But now there's a second one too.
In a way i suppose there's more space for me
But it feels more empty without you

I've always had one room
And now I'll have two
We wore matching gold bracelets
But now I wear two
And it'll suddenly just be me alone
When it's always been me and you

#47

same (but different)

My weight is the same
As it was when i came
My eyes remain a dark brown
And nor have i changed my name
My height is still five two
And I may have gotten too used to
Thinking of me as we
That though it seems like i have gone back the same
The truth is i left behind a huge part of me
Right there with you.

#48

LucIdiTy (lit)

i am out with a light
Searching for darkness
And in my bewildered search
i drank the entire bottle of medicine
Only to discover that too much was poison
In my bewildered search
i befriended the one who seeked to destroy me

And look where all this light has got me

So much light that it has blinded me

Blinded so I couldn't see

At the end of the day it was the darkness. that
guided me.

#49

Untitled

i remember when i fell
in love
(Or was it fell apart ?)
i can't quite recall
but it elicited an ineffable pang
Deeply hidden in my heart

And the tempests hit us fast,
(As if we could ever last)
if you were a glass,
Then I was a wall-
For you were meant to shatter
while i stood through it all.

And now you burn me at your stake-
Claiming "she's a witch in our wake".
But Darling, you can't kill a phoenix with fire
just as truth can't heal a liar.
So I rise from the ashes
As who i am; whole
(But covered with gashes.)

Unlike you, when i broke
i didnt break others
i just- -

Your breath stilled beneath my hand,
And i stood, unmoving, waiting
for the relief to land
What if.. it wasn't you who fractured first—
What if i met your best with my worst?

A wall, untouched by storm or flame
Tall, unyielding, you could never get through
But maybe walls carry the strain too-
Hairline fractures, spreading beneath,
Hiding until the breaking point is reached.

At the final hour,
with you cold at my feet
(i still feel incomplete.)
I wonder if I struck because i had to—
Or because
I was broken too.

Two broken people

Each with bits of a heart,

I used to think we'd fallen in love

But maybe we'd
just
fallen
apart.

#50

A letter

To our loving educational system

I wear airpods now
They're very efficient
And dont get tangled.
Or ever lost; they have a tracker.

My AirPods can block out every noise around me
Leaving me perfectly alone.
They're very sleek. And quite advanced.

But days when
My work is overflowing
My mind is overworked
My tears are just falling

I am once again Reduced
to my
Old battered
Tangled

Wired
Earphones

That could always get lost
And never completely isolate me
The ones that had such a..
Delicate old love about them.

I am expected to work like my AirPods.
And i try i do really.
Constant efficiency. Easy. Can block out others.
Someone. Always. Knows. Where. I. Am.

But some days
I become.
Like my tangled

Wired

Earphones.

Some days

I become
Human.

* * * * *A Special Segment of Thoughts i Couldn't Finish* * * * *

i. does the bottle support the water / or does the water
give the Bottle purpose?

ii. & i was afraid of the ocean so,
because with a heart so heavy, I was bound to drown.

iii. Your tears wrote the code in my brain
you say stay away
but how can i refrain.

THE END

And from drops of poetry
from here & there
i've formed an ocean
in the middle of nowhere

www.ingramcontent.com/pod-product-compliance
Lightning Source LLC
LaVergne TN
LVHW041128150826
845673LV00007B/2224

* 9 7 9 8 8 9 6 7 3 4 7 4 1 *